Jazz Piano Vocabulary

Volume 4
The Lydian Mode

by Roberta Piket

With additional material available
on-line at www.muse-eek.com

Muse Eek Publishing Company
New York, New York

Copyright © 2003 by Roberta Piket. All rights reserved

ISBN 1594899568

No part of this publication may be reproduced, stored in a
retrieval system, or transmitted, in any form or by any means,
electronic, mechanical, photocopying, recording, or otherwise,
without the prior written permission of the publisher.

Printed in the United States

This publication can be purchased from your local bookstore or by contacting:
Muse Eek Publishing Company
P.O. Box 509
New York, NY 10276, USA
Phone: 212-473-7030
Fax: 212-473-4601
http://www.muse-eek.com
sales@muse-eek.com

Table Of Contents

Acknowledgements	*iv*
About the Author	*v*
Foreword	*vi*
How to Use This Book	*vii*
Swung Eighth Notes	*viii*
Order of Presentation	*viii*
Fingering	*viii*
Introduction to the Lydian Mode	9
Applying The Lydian Mode To Improvisation	10
Major Seventh Chord	10
Major Seventh #11 ("Sharp Eleven") Chord	11
#11 and ♭5 Chords	12
Left-Hand Chords and Fourths-Based Voicings	13
Two-Handed Major 7#11 Voicings	16
Enharmonic Spellings	16
Lydian Modes: Fingerings and Left Hand Chord Voicings	18
Hand Position	18
Practice Method	18
Dynamics	19
Using The Left-Hand Chord Voicings	19
Swung Eighth Notes, Articulation and Phrasing	19
The Modes	20
Phrasing and Comping: A Rhythmic Approach	23
A Phrasing Exercise	23
Getting Control Of Your Left Hand	24
Examples From the Masters	26
Comping Patterns	28
Rhythmic Comping Patterns in 3	28
Jazz Etude: *Just A Waltz*	32
Keeping The Form	32
Further Exploration	37
Post-Modern Jazz Harmony and Composition Sampler	37
What Next?	38

Acknowledgments

The author gratefully acknowledges Bruce Arnold and Muse Eek Publishing for the opportunity to publish this book.

The author would also like to thank pianist Mike Garson for permission to use his beautiful artwork.

Special thanks to Billy Mintz for his support and encouragement.

About the Author

Pianist/keyboardist Roberta Piket is from Queens, NY. Her father, composer Frederick Piket, gave her her first piano lessons when she was seven years old. Roberta began playing seriously in her early teens, studying jazz piano with Walter Bishop, Jr and classical piano with Vera Wels. After graduating from prestigious Hunter College High School, she entered the joint double-degree program at Tufts University and the New England Conservatory of Music, earning a Bachelor's Degree in Computer Science from the former and a Bachelor's Degree in Jazz Studies from the latter. During this time she studied privately with Fred Hersch, Stanley Cowell, Jim McNeely and Bob Moses. Soon after graduation Roberta returned to New York City to devote herself to music full-time, which she has done ever since. In New York, she studied for six years with Richie Beirach and also studied briefly with Sofia Rosoff.

Roberta has performed professionally as a sidewoman with David Liebman, Rufus Reid, Michael Formanek, Lionel Hampton, Mickey Roker, Harvey Wainapel, Eliot Zigmund, Billy Mintz, and the BMI/New York Jazz Orchestra, and has twice been a featured guest on *Marian McPartland's Piano Jazz*, on National Public Radio.

Roberta has taught at Long Island University and has several private students at the Berkeley-Carroll School in Brooklyn. She has also held master classes and/or clinics at the Eastman School of Music, Rutgers University, Duke University, Cal Arts, as well as many other institutions in the U.S., Europe, and Japan.

Roberta has six CDs as a leader which have frequently made the jazz magazines' yearly top ten lists. *Piano & Keyboard* recently called Roberta "one of the most accomplished and inventive young jazz pianists currently working on the scene."

More information about Roberta's music as well as downloadable tracks and lead sheets can be found at her web sites: www.RobertaJazz.com and www.AlternatingCurrent.info.

Foreword

Many instrumentalists wish to pursue jazz improvisation, but are intimidated because they don't know what notes to play over chord changes, beyond the chord tones themselves. Frequently students who do know what scales they need to learn in order to play over changes are unable to internalize this information to the point of being able to use the scales in an actual playing situation. They may have difficulty learning the notes because they are unsure of what fingerings to use, or they may not have had enough guidance in making the transition from *playing* the scales to *applying* them in a playing situation.

This book provides specific details on practicing the Lydian mode in all twelve keys and applying it to jazz improvisation. You will also find exercises to help you improve your phrasing and comping, an original Lydian mode etude, and, since fingering is often an issue for less experienced pianists, fingerings for every scale in the book. The goal is to provide you with enough guidance to work confidently on your own so that you can integrate the Lydian mode into your playing while improving other aspects of your playing.

The Lydian is often considered a more "advanced mode" because it is used with more complex chord structures that do not appear naturally in the diatonic scales, such as the maj7#11. Before you begin this book, if you are new to improvisation, you may wish to start with one of the following books in this series: Volume 1 (the Major scale); Volume 2 (the Dorian mode) or Volume 5 (the Mixolydian mode). If you are already fluent with using those scales to improvise, then you are ready for this book. In this volume, you will learn to use the Lydian mode to create voicings and lines that transcend the bebop language that we have discussed in those other books. Like the other books in this series, this book offers a workbook to jazz improvisation with specific exercises that you can practice. You can listen to these examples on the Muse Eek website as well.

This book is part of a series (available as e-books or in paper format) that focus on learning and applying jazz scales in order to give you the vocabulary and skill to become a fluid jazz improvisor.

Muse Eek Publishing has created a website with a FAQ forum for this book. If you get stuck, or have questions or feedback, please contact me at Roberta@muse-eek.com and I will be happy to respond in the forum.

Roberta Piket
Brooklyn, New York

How To Use This Book

This series of books assumes that you know how to read music and that you have a basic understanding of major scales. If you need to brush up on your note-reading or the diatonic (major and minor) system, there are lessons on this topic in the members area of the publisher's website. If you find anything in this book confusing, please visit the Muse Eek web site at www.muse-eek.com first and check the FAQ section for this book to see if your question has already been answered. If not, use the form on the website to e-mail your questions.

A note on terminology: Occasionally the word *scale* will be used in this book interchangeably with the word *mode*. Generally I will only use the word *scale* when discussing general concepts such as scale tones or sequencing through a scale. When discussing a specific mode (such as D Lydian, for example) I will use the word *mode*.

The purpose of this book is to help you improve your ability to improvise using the Lydian mode and to learn how to use this mode to navigate chords such as major 7th#11 and major 7th♭5 chords. While learning these modes, you will also gain knowledge that will help you to become a better player in general, such as how to comp and phrase and how to build fourths-based voicings. Hopefully you have already mastered the scales found in Volumes 1, 2 and 5 of this series (the Major scale, Dorian mode, and Mixolydian mode respectively) before approaching this volume. If not, you may wish to learn that material first. This is because the harmony that is dealt with in those volumes is more fundamental to a knowledge of jazz piano harmony than the Lydian mode, as important as it is.

You may wish to use a metronome to be certain that you are not slowing down on difficult passages. If you are able, try putting the metronome on the "two and four"; that is, the second and fourth beats of each measure. This emphasis on the "weak" beats instead of the "strong" first and third beats is part of what gives jazz its unique rhythmic character. If it is too difficult for you to play with the metronome on two and four, then first learn the scales with the metronome on the quarter note and then, after you are comfortable with the notes, try the "two and four" again. Eventually it will get easier to feel the music this way and your sense of rhythm will become stronger and more sophisticated.

This book contains a great deal of material. You will not be able to learn everything in the book in one sitting. In fact, depending on your background, and how much time you choose to dedicate to the piano, it may take you anywhere from a few weeks to several months or more to truly master the exercises in this book. Spend as much time as you need on each page before moving on to the next. You do not have to wait until you have mastered all twelve of the Lydian modes before beginning the other exercises in this book. You can practice those exercises over the modes that you have already learned, adding to the exercises as your vocabulary grows.

Consistency is critical. Even if you have less time on some days than on other days, it is extremely important that you refresh your memory almost every day until the material is completely engrained. If you do this, you will find that you will progress much more quickly and will save yourself a great deal of frustration.

Swung Eighth Notes

As in the previous volumes in this series, each scale is presented in an eighth note pattern (resolving to a quarter note at the top and bottom) to allow for an even four-bar phrase as the scale ascends and descends. By now you should be comfortable playing each exercise with *swung eighth notes*. Recall that in swung (or "swinging") eighth notes, the first eighth note in a pair of eight notes is held longer than the second eighth note, giving the notes a relaxed triplet feel.

Order of Presentation

The exercises and sample melodies are ordered by key using the *circle of fifths*. The circle of fifths allows us to progress through all the keys by moving either up or down in perfect fifths from one key to the next. Only by moving up or down in fifths can we go through all the keys without repeating any key.

In this book we will progress up in fifths, from F Lydian to C Lydian to G Lydian, etc., until we arrive at the last mode, B♭ Lydian. (We will start with F Lydian because it has no sharps or flats.)

Fingering

Often inexperienced pianists find it difficult to know which finger to use on which key. The fingerings that are provided in this book are intended to keep you from "running out of fingers" as you play ascending and descending lines.

Fortunately, fingering notation for piano is standardized throughout all genres of music. The thumb of each hand is always "1", and the pinky is always "5". If you can remember this then you will quickly become proficient at applying the correct fingerings as you learn to play a passage of written music.

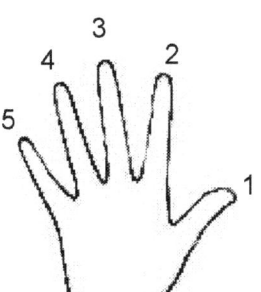 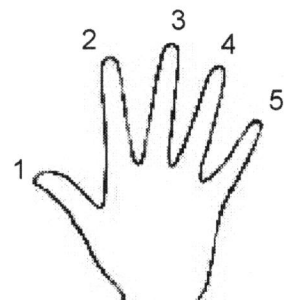

Particularly if you are self-taught, some of these fingerings may at first seem awkward. Give yourself a chance to get used to them. After learning them, if something still feels awkward, you can change it. Everyone's hand is different. However, don't assume they don't work if they feel "funny" the first time you try them. Practice them slowly, making sure to apply them accurately and consistently. Only by applying the correct fingerings every time you play will using them become automatic. Eventually, with enough experience, you will be able to determine the correct fingering on your own.

Introduction To The Lydian Mode

The modes that developed in Europe during the Medieval period are sometimes known as the "Church modes" because they evolved through the use of Gregorian chant, the sacred monophonic music of Europe's Catholic Church during this period. These modes are derived from the Major scale. Each mode has the same notes as the Major scale, but each mode starts and ends on a different note from the Major scale. The seven modes that we use in jazz are: Ionian, Dorian, Lydian, Lydian, Mixolydian, Aeolian, and Locrian.

The focus of this book is the Lydian mode. The Lydian mode is frequently used instead of the major scale for soloing over major 7th and major 7th♯11 chords.

The Lydian mode can be derived by starting on the fourth note of any Major scale and playing the notes of that Major scale. For example, F is the fourth note of the C Major scale. The F Lydian mode starts and ends on F and contains all the notes of the C Major scale:

F lydian Mode

Because the F Lydian mode uses the notes of the C Major scale, C Major is referred to as the *parent scale* of F Lydian. By knowing the parent scale of a mode, it is easy to figure out the notes that belong to that mode. As another example, if we want to play a D Lydian mode, we would first want to understand that D is the fourth degree of the A Major scale, making A Major the parent scale of D Lydian. Thus, the D Lydian mode starts and ends on D and contains all the notes found in the A Major scale:

D Lydian Mode

Another way to think of the Lydian mode is in terms of its sequence of whole steps and half steps. The pattern for any Lydian mode is:

F Lydian Interval Pattern

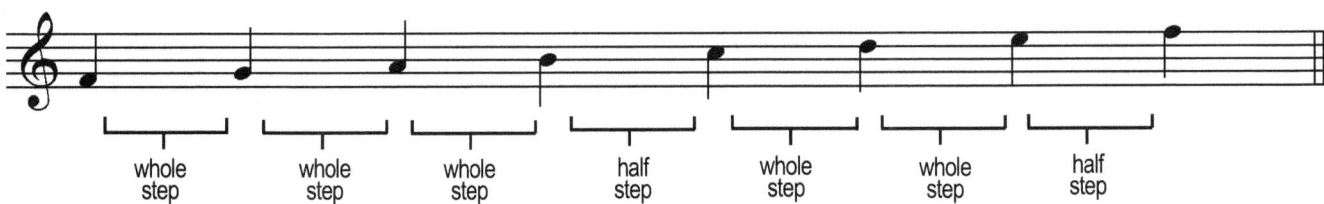

Perhaps the simplest and easiest way to think of the Lydian mode is as a Major scale with the fourth degree raised by a half step:

Keep this "raised fourth" concept in mind as you read through the next few pages.

Applying The Lydian Mode To Improvisation

There are two chords to which the Lydian mode is commonly applied. We will discuss each of these below.

Major Seventh Chord

If you worked out of Volume One of this series (*The Major Scale*) you learned how to improvise over a major 7th chord using the major scale. In Volume One, you will recall that in the major scale, the fourth degree is considered an "avoid note" (i.e., a note that should only be used as a passing tone resolving to a chord tone or a color tone).

If we raise the fourth degree of the major scale, as we do to derive the Lydian scale, we eliminate this "avoid" note. Play the previous example and the following example to hear the difference:

C Lydian Scale played over C Major 7th (no avoid note)

The Lydian scale can also be used over a major 7th chord (or over a major triad or a $^6_9$ chord, both of which are closely releated). As noted above, the Lydian scale contains almost the same notes as the major scale, the exception being the fourth degree, which is raised in the Lydian scale.

(Note: The jazz composer George Russell wrote a seminal book and developed a complete theoretical system around the concept that the Lydian scale is a more appropriate scale than the major scale for over a major chord. The details of this system are beyond the scope of this book. The interested reader is referred to <u>The Lydian Chromatic Concept Of Tonal Organization</u>, originally published in 1959; republished in 2001 by Concept Publishing.)

Major Seventh ♯11 ("Sharp Eleven") Chord

As you can see in the C Major scale below, the 4th degree of the major scale is the same note as the eleventh, down an octave.

The following example illustrates the chord tones and possible upper extensions in a C major 7th♯11 chord and how they correspond to the Lydian scale:

C major 7th#11 Chord Tones and Upper Extensions

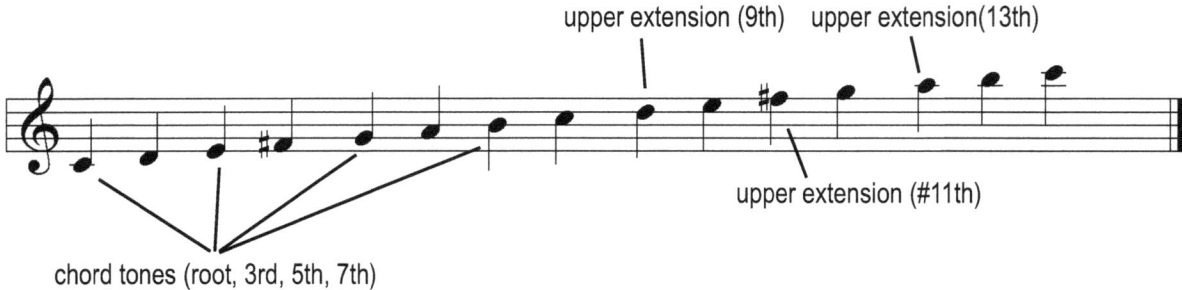

#11 and ♭5 Chords

You can see from this example that all Lydian scale tones will work over a major 7th#11 chord There are no avoid notes.

Frequently students ask what the difference is between a #11 and a ♭5, since they represent the same note. When a specific voicing is not specified, as, for example, in a simple leadsheet with only a melody and chord symbols, the ♭5 implies that there is no natural 5th in the chord. This is because in Be-bop, natural and altered versions of the same upper extension generally do not exist in the same chord. (Note that the bass note in parentheses is only provided so that you can hear the chord against its root when playing it.)

Example 1

By contrast, the #11 symbol allows for the possibility that there is a natural 5th in the chord:

Example 2

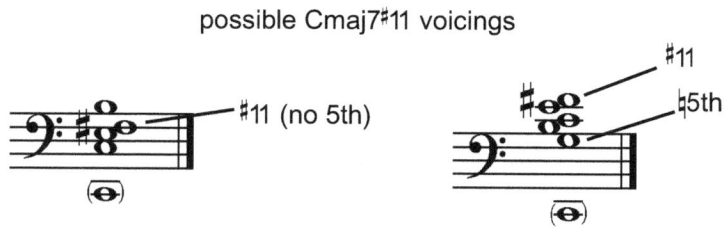

Because a chord with a ♭5 cannot contain the natural 5, in theory we would not use the Lydian scale over it, since the Lydian scale does contain the natural 5. However, in practice, the symbols "♭5" and "♯11" are frequently used interchangeably, and often it *is* appropriate to use the Lydian mode over a major 7th♭5 chord. When you see a major 7th♭5 chord, a good rule of thumb is: if the chord and melody do not specify a ♯5, then it is okay to have a natural 5 in the sound and therefore the Lydian mode can be used.

Left-Hand Chords and Fourths-Based Voicings

Once you are comfortable playing the Lydian mode in a given key with your right hand, the next step is to learn the corresponding chords in the left hand. The goal is to be able to play these left-hand voicings while playing the mode in the right hand. Left-hand voicings are illustrated with each scale for the major 7th chord and the major 7th♯11 chord.

Major Seventh Chord

In previous volumes of this series, including Volumes One and Two, we used left-hand voicings stacked in thirds, using the 3rd, 5th 7th and 9th of the chord, such as in this C major 7th voicing:

Example 3

Left-hand chord voicing built in 3rds

In this volume, we are going to learn another major seventh chord voicing that is based instead on *fourths*. Technically this chord is not a major 7th chord. It is known as a $^6_9$ ("six nine") chord because it consists of the 3rd, 6th (or thirteenth) and natural 9th of the chord. However, this chord is often used interchangeably with a major 7th chord.

In forming voicings based on thirds, we ascend a given scale in thirds. Whether a given third is major or minor is determined by which third is in the scale that we are using. Similarly, to form a voicing based on fourths, we ascend from a given scale tone in fourths. Each fourth will be either perfect, diminished or augmented, depending on which tone is present in the scale we are using.

For the $^6_9$ voicing, we will begin on the third of the chord. Ascending from the third in fourths and holding the tones to the Lydian scale results in two perfect 4ths:

Example 4

F$^6_9$ left-hand chord voicing built in Fourths

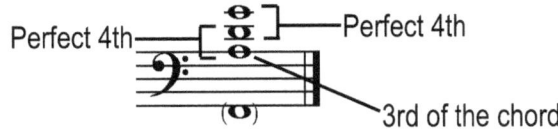

Fourths give our voicing a different sound from the third-based voicings we've been using. This voicing is provided in the scales section for each mode.

Major Seventh #11 Chord

Let's examine a common 4th-based left-hand voicing for a Major 7th #11 chord. This voicing contains the root, #11th and 7th of the chord:

Example 5

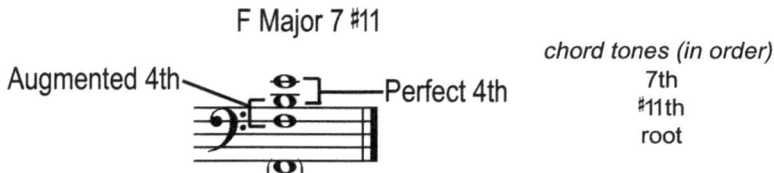

In this voicing, we use the F Lydian mode to ascend in fourths from F, the root of the chord. There is more tension in this voicing than in the $^6_9$ voicing, however, because of the augmented 4th on the bottom (the interval from F to B). (The first note up from F has to be a B because B is the scale tone a fourth above F that is contained in the F Lydian mode. A perfect 4th instead would make this note a B♭ which does not exist in the F Lydian mode.

Fourths-based voicing can sometimes sound rather ascetic and dry. You can frequently add other intervals, such as a third, for a fuller sound:

Example 6

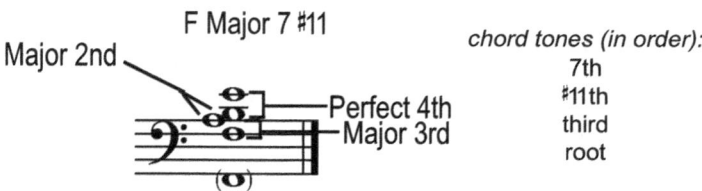

Whether to add the third to this voicing is a matter of taste. In the scales section, the major 7 #11 voicing provided has the third in it.

When a voicing is too high, we can invert the chord to place it in a better range. For example, in the scales section of this book, under the the A Lydian scale, the A major 7 #11 voicing looks like this:

Example 7

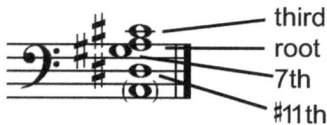

A Major 7 #11 inverted

As you can see, the 3rd is on top. This same inversion on an F major 7#11 chord would look like this:

Example 8

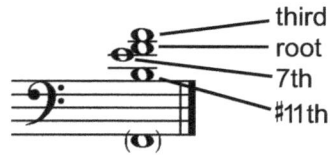

F Major 7 #11 inverted

Evidently, not all inversions will work in all keys. Some will either be too low and muddy, or too high.

It is extremely beneficial to practice all the left-hand voicings in *all possible* inversions. This will give you a greater variety of sounds and more flexibility in comping for yourself, no matter where your right hand is on the keyboard. Play all inversions of the chords in this section up and down the keyboard for two octaves each to learn them. To get you started, here is what this exercise would look like when practiced on an F major 7th#11 chord.

Example 9

You can hear a sound sample of this example at the Muse-Eek website under this book's title page. This will give you an idea of how the exercise should sound when played smoothly and correctly.

Two-Handed Major 7#11 Voicings

In the previous section, we added a third to the chord we built in fourths. If we move that third up an octave, we are stacking another 4th on top of the voicing:

Example 10

We can add another fourth on top, which corresponds to the 13th of the chord, and optionally add even another fourth, the 9th:

Example 11

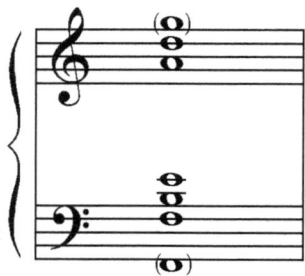

We can use these two-handed voicings when comping for another instrumentalist.

You can build voicings on fourths based on other scales or modes you know such as Major, Dorian, and Mixolydian by starting on a chord or scale tone, and going up in fourths, staying within the tones of the scale.

Play through the chords of some of the tunes that you know, working out voicings by stacking the corresponding scale tones in fourths.

Enharmonic Spellings

The inexperienced reader may be put off by examples that contain unusual note spellings such as the E# in the following:

Using "E#" instead of "F natural" is the correct way to write this chord because E is the 11th of the chord. Raising an E gives us E#. However, frequently you might see this voicing written with an F natural instead of an E# because it is easier to read:

In the scales section of this book, the correct enharmonic spelling (in the above example, E#) is always used because it makes the pattern of intervals in the voicing clearer. The first example makes it evident that the distance between the bottom two notes of the rootless voicing is a perfect fourth, while the second example does not make this as visible. Since understanding the intervallic pattern of the voicing is part of learning the voicing, seeing it illustrated in this way consistently is helpful. If you are not familiar with them, you will quickly get used to reading unusual enharmonic spellings such as E# or C♭.

Lydian Modes: Fingerings And Left Hand Chord Voicings

Before you start learning the Lydian mode in all keys, here are a few suggestions and guidelines to help you get the most out of your practice time. If you remember these suggestions from the other volumes of this series you can skip this section and go right to the scales.

Hand Position

It is important to develop good habits with respect to hand position. It may not seem important when playing slowly, but when you begin to execute faster passages, you will find that good hand and wrist position will make a difference in your control, thus effecting your ability to play evenly and cleanly.

When playing notes that are close together, as is the case with scales, fingers should be curved, so that you are playing with the balls of your fingers. (If you have long finger nails you will need to cut them to achieve this.) All fingers should be kept in this rounded position whether you are using them or not. (See the picture below.) Of course if you are playing a widely spread chord, your fingers will not be as bent as they are when playing a scale in which each note is adjacent to the next note to be played. The idea is to keep your fingers in a gently bent yet relaxed position.

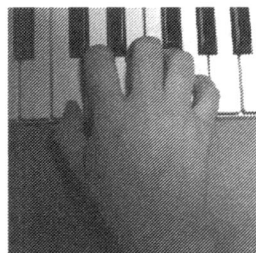

Many inexperienced pianists veer their wrists from side to side, particularly when changing hand position as they go up and down the keyboard while playing a scale. In medical circles this is known as ulnar deviation and is a great way to develop wrist tendonitis (a bad thing). When changing hand position as you ascend or descend the keyboard, do NOT change your wrist position relative to your hand. Instead, as your arm glides up (or down) the keyboard, bring your thumb under you hand and reach for the note. Let your thumb do the stretching, not your wrist. Keep your elbows close to your side.

Practice Method

To begin, practice each scale in the right hand, up two octaves and down two octaves, paying attention to the fingering provided. (Right hand fingering is notated above each note of the scale.) You may find it useful to say each note out loud as you play. Even better for your ear is to try to sing the notes of each scale while playing.

Once you learn the notes to a scale you will accompany yourself with the appropriate chords in your left hand, much as your left hand would "comp" while your right hand solos. As a matter of training and technique, however, it is valuable to master all the Lydian modes with both hands. For this purpose, left hand fingerings for each Lydian mode are provided (below each note).

Dynamics

Keep in mind that the left hand is *accompanying* the right hand. Therefore, the left hand should be a bit softer in volume than the right hand. At first it may seem difficult to coordinate your hands in this way, but if you try to *hear* the right hand melody louder, as opposed to merely trying to play harder with your right hand, then eventually you will naturally begin to emphasize the melody more.

Using The Left-Hand Chord Voicings

Once you are comfortable playing a given scale in your right hand, the next step is to play the corresponding voicing in the left hand along with the scale in the right hand. As discussed in the previous section, it is suggested that you practice all twelve of the Lydian modes against the major 7th#11 chord; then practice all the Lydian modes again, this time against the $\frac{6}{9}$ chord. This will reinforce the sound of the harmony in your ear and your brain. You can also practice the modes with any major 7th chord voicing with which you are familar, including root position as well as rootless voicings.

The bass note in parentheses below the chord indicates the root of the chord. While in general you would not play this note in an actual playing situation, it is useful to hear the root when practicing. Play the root with your left hand and sustain it with the damper (sustain) pedal, then lift your hand and play the first rootless voicing (the major 7th#11 chord) as written. While holding this chord with your left hand, take your foot off the damper (sustain) pedal and play the scale in your right hand. This technique will help you hear the chord from the bottom up, allowing you to get its tonality in your ear. It will also enable you to aurally relate the scale to the chord. (Note: This is for practice only. Do not play and hold the root in an actual playing situation.) When playing a major 7th#11 chord, identify each chord tone in your mind as root, 3rd, #11 or 7th.

After you have gone through this process for all twelve of the major 7th#11 voicings, repeat the same steps with the second voicing for all twelve of the $\frac{6}{9}$ chords. The second chord is notated in the second measure for legibility only. You should play this chord the same way that you played the major 7th#11 chord, holding down the chord and then playing the entire scale in your right hand up and down two octaves.

Swung Eighth Notes, Articulation and Phrasing

As discussed in previous volumes of this series, play these scales with a swung eighth note feel.

As you become more comfortable with the actual notes of each scale and chord, you should begin to focus more on the subtleties of articulation. Each scale should be played legato, meaning that the notes are connected. Many jazz piano students make the mistake of trying to play too staccato (disconnected and short), because of the percussive nature of jazz. However, in trying to play legato, do *not* use the damper (sustain) pedal when playing medium tempo or faster jazz eighth note lines. This is another common error made by inexperienced pianists.

You can hear these scales played correctly with the proper articulation and swing feel at this book's title page at the Muse-Eek website.

The Modes

F Lydian mode

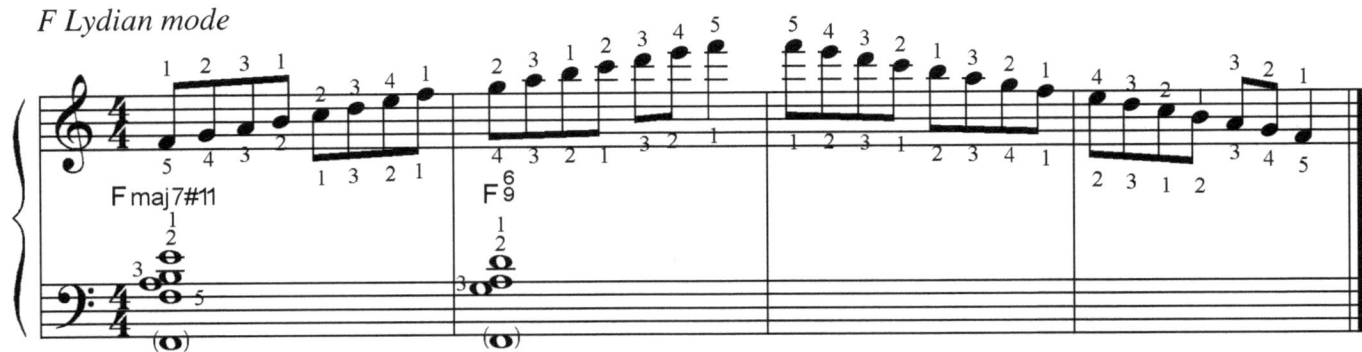

C Lydian mode

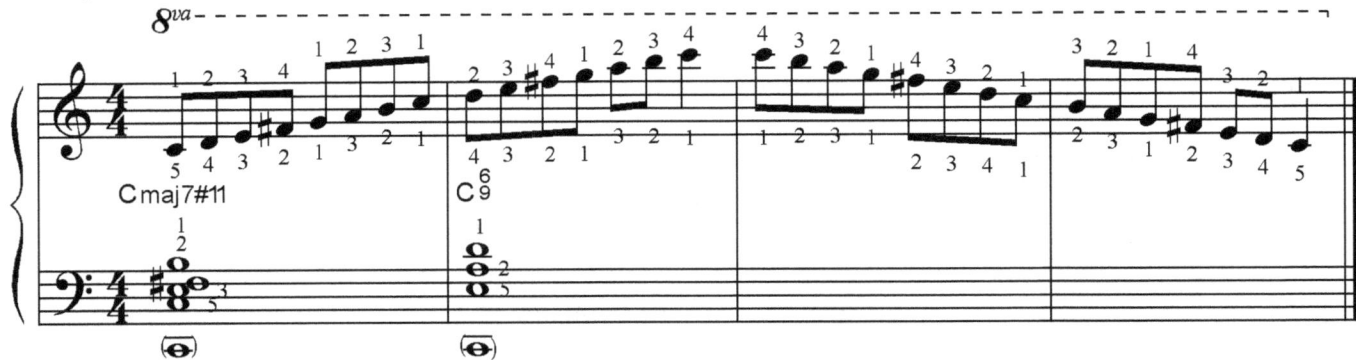

G Lydian mode

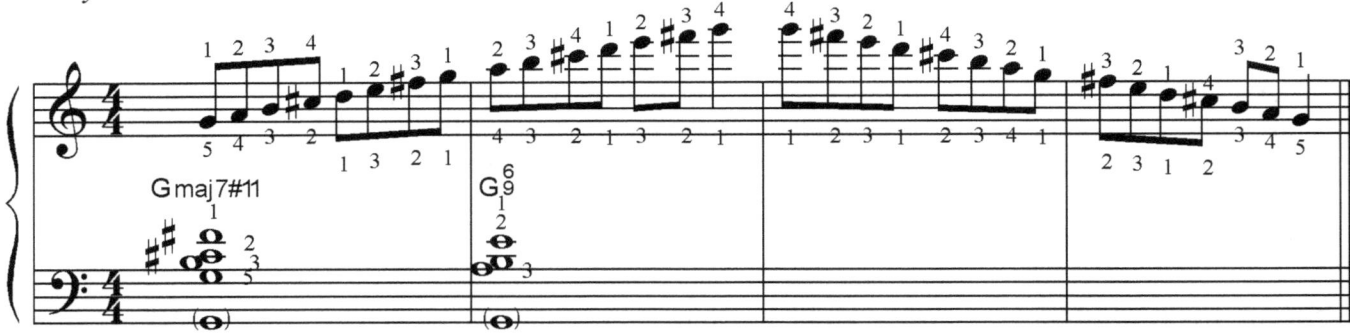

D Lydian mode

A Lydian mode

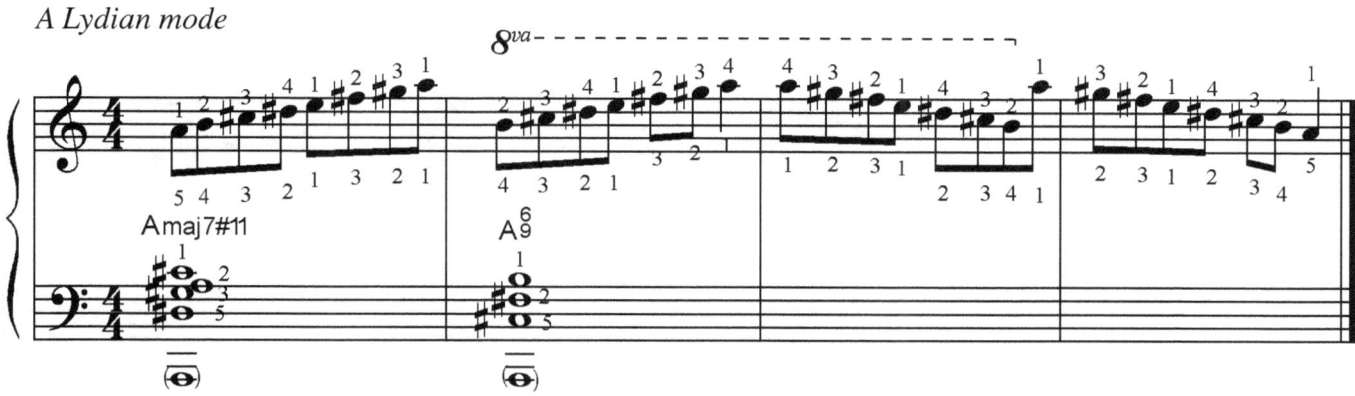

E Lydian mode

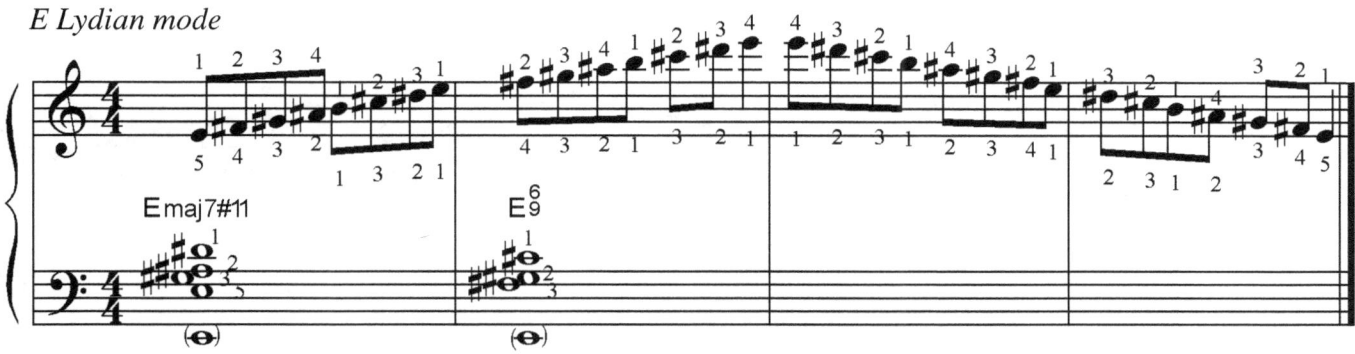

B Lydian mode

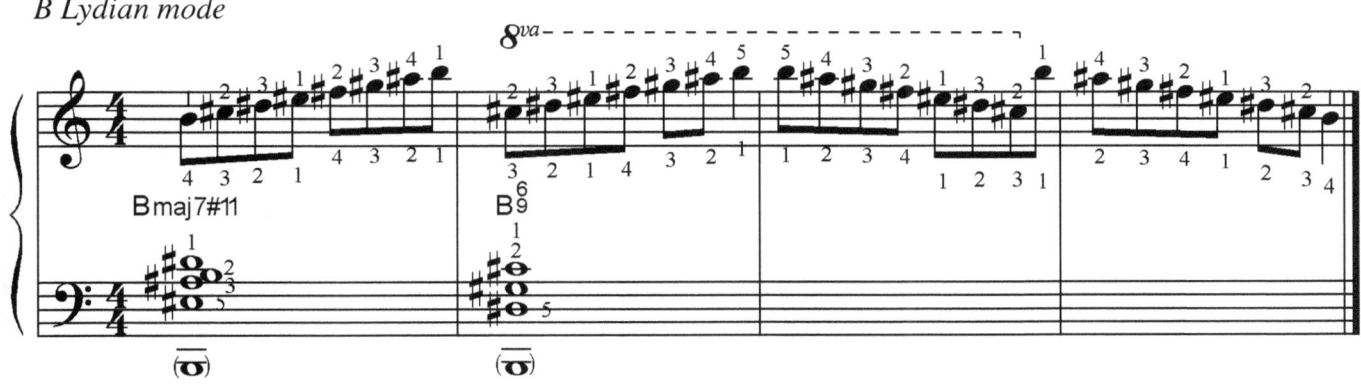

G♭ Lydian

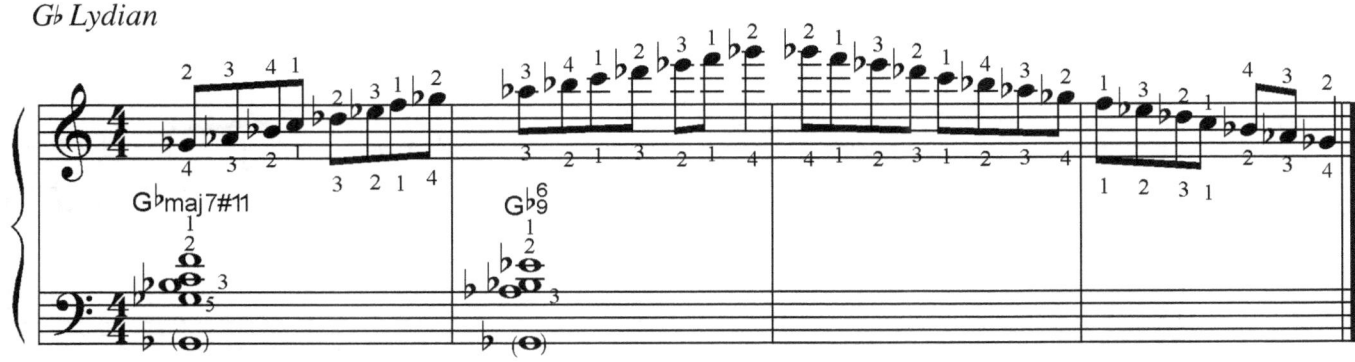

D♭ Lydian mode

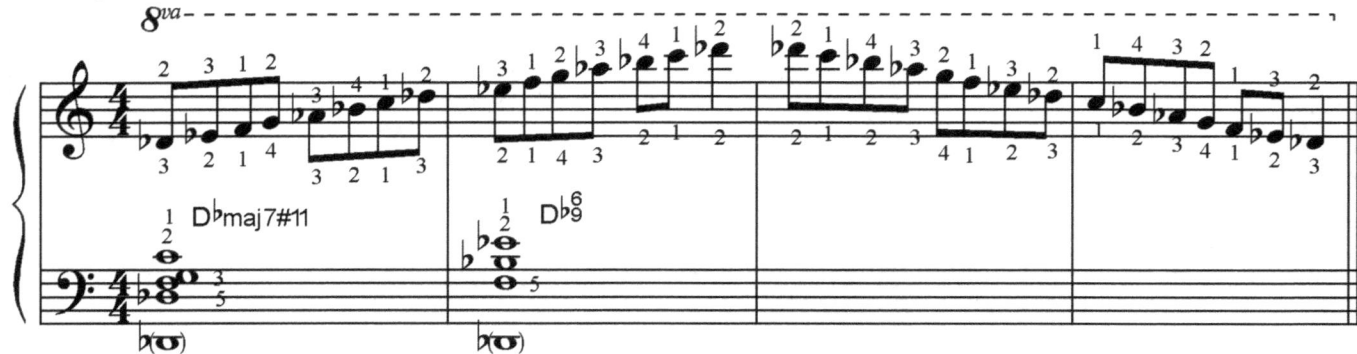

Note: For this scale you can also use the same left hand fingering as the Eb Lydian mode, if preferred.

A♭ Lydian mode

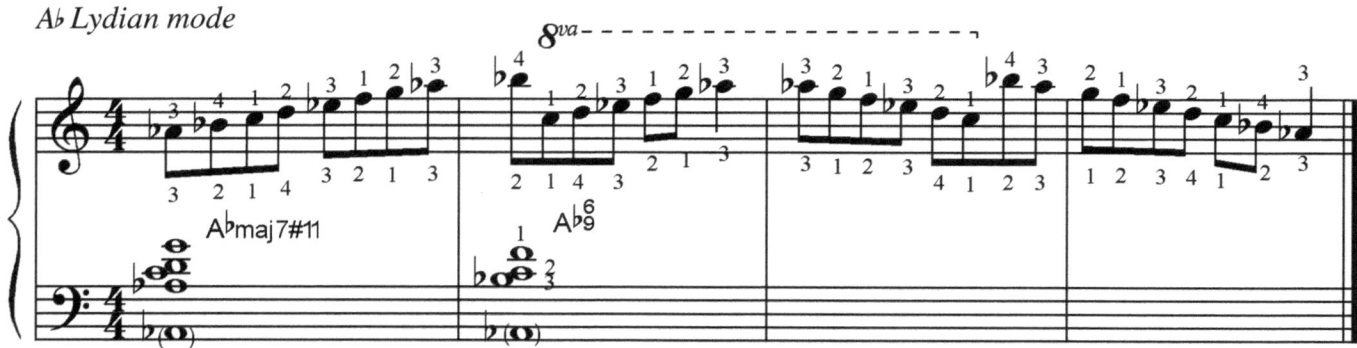

Note: For this scale you can also use the same left hand fingering as the Eb Lydian mode, if preferred.

E♭ Lydian mode

B♭ Lydian mode

Phrasing and Comping: A Rhythmic Approach

Phrasing Exercise

When I teach, one issue that comes up frequently, even with some relatively experienced improvisors, is that of phrasing. Try a little experiment: Record yourself improvising over a tune that you are comfortable with for a chorus or two. Now listen back. Does your solo consist of an ongoing string of notes with no discernible phrases, and no "breathing room"? If so, then you need to think about expressing your ideas in musical phrases, and leaving space between the phrases.

One reason piano players may neglect to leave space is that playing steadily without stopping is a way of beating out the tempo for themselves. There are at least a few problems with this approach. Playing lines without phrasing is a little like talking in run-on sentences. It doesn't make much sense and people tend to lose interest in what you are saying. Additionally, if you take breaks between your phrases, you have a chance to think about and "hear" what you want to play next. For this reason, the quality and clarity of your ideas will be higher. Finally, you must learn to feel the beat of the music no matter what you are playing, or even if you're not playing at all.

Following is an exercise that will help you improve your phrasing. You can apply this exercise to the Lydian mode, or you can apply it to any chord progression or scale you like.

We will start by playing over a single chord. This way you can focus on the exercise, instead of being distracted by dealing with many chord changes that you may not be entirely comfortable with. I have chosen C major7th#11, but if you feel more comfortable using a different chord, that is fine.

Set your metronome to about half note = 60 (or quarter note =120) to begin with. If you feel comfortable doing so, set the metronome so that it only clicks on the '2' and '4' of each measure. (If this is not comfortable for you, don't worry about it right now. It is something you should practice separately, or with this exercise after you get comfortable with the exercise itself.)

Now comes the challenging part. Solo over your chord progression, for two bars, then rest while counting two more bars. You will continue on in this way, playing a two-bar phrase, and then not playing for two bars. Play simple, melodic eighth-note lines. Below is an example of what such an improvisation might sound like. (In this example the notes have *not* been limited to the Lydian scale; we are incorporating the chromaticism that normally occurs in Be-bop through the use of chromatic approach notes. For more on approach notes, please see *Jazz Piano Vocabulary - Volume 5: The Mixolydian Mode*.) You can use whatever notes you are comfortable with for this exercise. The focus for this exercise is your phrasing.

Example 12

An audio file of this example can be found on the Muse-Eek web site under this book's title. Additionally, you will find a MIDI file of piano comping over C major 7th#11. You can adjust the tempo of this file and use it to practice this exercise repeatedly. Remember: when you do this exercise, whether it is with the MIDI file or with your metronome, use the right hand only. Do not comp for yourself.

Getting Control Of Your Left Hand

Another problem that some pianists have is that the left hand gets in the way while the right hand is soloing. That is why I have suggested you do the above exercise with the right hand only. The left hand tends to act as a rhythmic crutch, helping you keep the time or find "one". Often it gets in the way of the flow of the right hand's lines.

Here is an exercise to help you learn to use your left hand judiciously and to avoid banging it down on the first beat of every measure or "treading water" on every upbeat, common problems among pianists.

Choose any upbeat within a measure. We are going to comp with the left hand only on that upbeat. For example, if we chose the "and" of '3', our left-hand comping pattern would look like this:

(We've used "slash notation" instead of actual note heads because you can do this exercise with any chord or chord progression.) Play this comping rhythm with the metronome set as slow as necessary for you to play it correctly. Start with the metronome on every quarter note. (When that feels comfortable you can try setting it to click on "two" and "four".) After you get comfortable playing this pattern over a single chord, the next step is to try play over it with your right hand. Here is an example of what that might sound like if we play this exercise over a C major 7th#11 chord. An audio file of this example can be found on the Muse-Eek web site:

Example 13

Now let's try applying this pattern to a short vamp. Once you can play the changes in your left hand on the "and" of '3', try to solo over this progression while keeping the left hand going.

A MIDI file consisting of a walking bass line over the above progression can be found on the Muse-Eek website under this book's title. You can adjust the tempo and practice this exercise along with it. Or use your metronome.

Let's try the same exercise over the same progession, this time with the left hand comping on the "and" of '2'. Remember that you can use the same MIDI file as in the previous example to work on this:

The purpose of this exercise is to strengthen your rhythmic conception so that you can comp purposefully, placing your left hand where it is most appropriate in relation to the right hand phrases. (As with any practice exercise, it will sound mechanical to always comp on the same place in the measure, and you would not do this in an actual playing situation.)

Examples From the Masters

Great pianists have different approaches to comping. For example, Bill Evans often laid down his left hand to match the accents in his right hand lines, as in this recording of Peri's Scope (<u>We Will Meet Again</u>, *Warner*)

Example 14

Another comping approach Bill Evans used frequently is a "call and response" technique, in which the left and right hands answer each other instead of playing at the same time. Wynton Kelly also comped this way a great deal, as in this passage from *Freddie Freeloader* (Miles Davis, <u>Kind Of Blue,</u> Columbia). (The notes in parentheses are ghosted):

Example 15

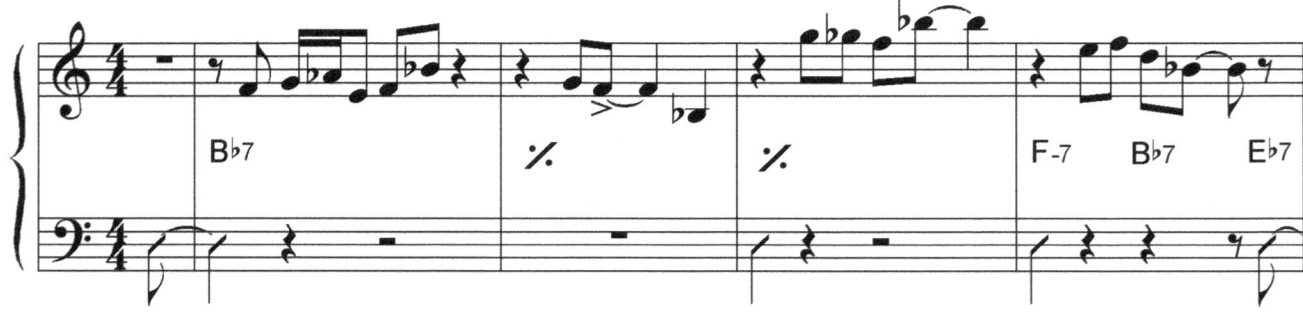

On some of his solos, Red Garland comped almost exclusively on the "and" of 2 and 4, as in this excerpt from the tune *Blues By Five*, on the Miles Davis CD, <u>Cookin'</u> (*Fantasy*):

Example 16

When you listen to jazz, pay attention to rhythmic aspects of the pianist's comping - where the chords fall in relation to both the measure and the melodic line.

The comping exercise above is a first step toward developing necessary hand independence and interdependence and strengthening your sense of rhythm and time. Your right hand lines will sound more flowing because your left hand will not be in the way.

This exercise may not come easily to you. In all its possible variations, you could easily spend a good year working on this, and it would be time well spent. However, even several minutes a day of this exercise will result in great improvement.

Comping Patterns

Below we will continue our discussion of comping and examine some specific comping rhythms you can use. Since all of the examples and practice material we've seen so far have been in $\frac{4}{4}$ meter. Let's look at some ways to get started comping in $\frac{3}{4}$ time. Play them with both hands together or with the left hand only. When you are comfortable, you can comp with the left hand and solo with the right hand at the same time.

Rhythmic Comping Patterns in 3

You are probably familiar with the following simple $\frac{3}{4}$ rhythmic pattern. (In this example, the bottom staff represents the bass, and the upper staff represents the chordal accompaniment:)

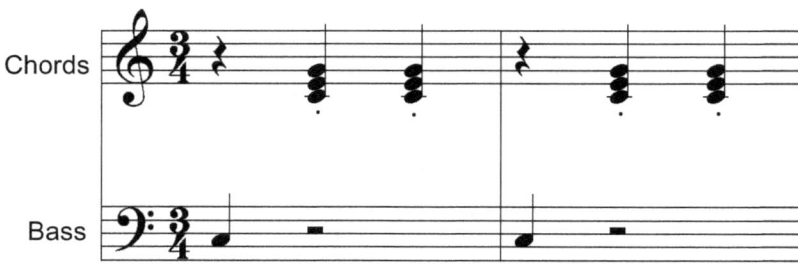

In jazz we do not use this pattern for comping because all of the chords fall on the downbeats, making it uninteresting. However, if we move the entire chordal accompaniment back by an eighth note so that it begins on the 'and' of 'one' instead of on 'two', the pattern takes on greater rhythmic interest. Play this rhythm on the piano using any chord progression you choose:

Example 17

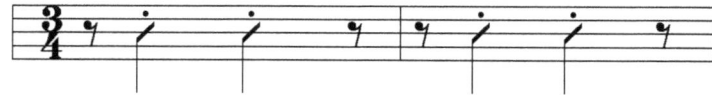

This process of moving a pattern over is called *rhythmic displacement*. Now let's displace the original pattern again. This time we will move it *forward* by an eight note:

Example 18

For simplicity and clarity of notation, let's rewrite this pattern without the ties.

Example 19

You may find these patterns challenging at first because they require you to play on the up-beats of the measure; that is, on the "ands" of the beats, rather than on the downbeats. In jazz, it is very important to be able to play on the upbeats. You should practice these patterns until you are comfortable enough with them to add your right hand. (Of course, you can also use them when you are comping for another instrument.)

Here is another interesting rhythmic pattern. This one consists of two dotted quarter notes.

Example 20

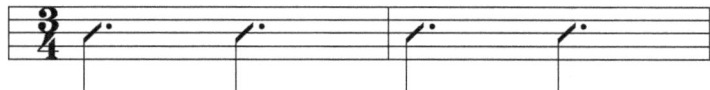

If we displace this pattern by moving it forward by one eighth-note we get this:

Example 21

In an actual playing situation, repeating the same pattern over and over sounds mechanical. In the "real world" you would want to mix and match, responding to the soloist and to the other members of the rhythm section. Practicing these rhythms, however, is an important intermediate step. Once you feel comfortable playing the different rhythmic patterns in this exercise, you will be better able to comp in a rhythmically fluid manner .

All of these patterns can be applied to other meters by adding rests to fill in the remainder of the measure. Here is our dotted half note pattern modified to fit in $\frac{4}{4}$ meter.

Example 22

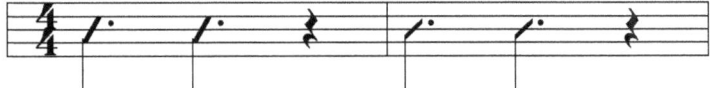

If we place a staccato over the first note of the pattern, we get a very common rhythm pattern in jazz known as the "Charleston" beat, named for the popular dance craze of the 1920's. Note that we are not changing the *rhythm* by adding the staccato, we are only changing the *articulation* of the notes.

Example 23

This rhythm is more commonly written as follows:

Example 24

If we shorten the articulation on the *second* beat instead of the first beat, you may recognize the result as the comping pattern used in the tune "Killer Joe", composed by Benny Golson:

Example 25

If we displace this rhythm by moving it forward by a quarter note, we get the following:

Example 26

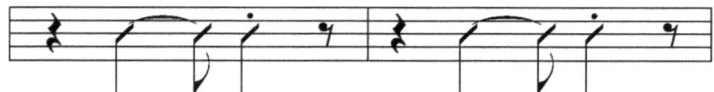

The rhythm above, with the following articulation, is the backbone of the Lee Morgan tune, *The Sidewinder*:

Example 27

As you can see, the "Charleston" beat can be used in many different ways in jazz. Find your own patterns in various meters, experimenting with different displacements and articulations, over tunes or changes with which you are familiar. Space is provided below for you to notate the comping patterns you find most interesting and useful. You can write out specific chord progressions, or use slash notation.

Jazz Etude: *Just A Waltz*

The harmony in this etude, composed by the author, focuses on the chords we have been working on in this book, but it also utilizes other chords with which you should be familiar by now. This piece will allow you to practice the harmonic material in this book, as well as several of the comping and phrasing concepts that have been discussed.

As you can see, this etude is in $\frac{3}{4}$ meter. The first two pages consist of a full grand staff piano part. You can play it as written, or you can interpret it as a leadsheet, simply playing the chord symbols provided along with the melody. Whichever way you interpret the chart, remember that the inner voicings should always be softer than the melody. This is a lyrical piece. Try to make the melody sing as you play. Also remember that it is a jazz waltz, which means you should *swing* the eighth notes.

Keeping The Form

Many less experienced players have trouble remembering where they are in the form of a tune. If you find yourself frequently getting lost in the form of this piece (or any piece you are working on), try repeating four bars at a time over and over. When you feel comfortable with four bars, try to play over eight bars at a time without losing your place. Keep trying to play larger chunks without getting lost. If you find your mind wandering, STOP, and start again. Critical to keeping the form is the ability to concentrate on the music in a relaxed but focused state, without allowing yourself to get distracted. You must also develop your internal sense of form to the point where you intuitively "feel" where you are in the musical form. If you practice consistently, both your ability to concentrate and your internal sense of form will improve greatly.

If you can read the full piano part, then you may find it useful to add these voicings to your vocabulary by transposing them into all twelve keys. The best way to do this is to play a voicing in all twelve keys through the circle of fifths, and then move on to the next chord.

In section B of *Just A Waltz* (marked "Blowing Changes"), a sample comping pattern is provided, illustrating what mixing and matching the comping patterns you have working on might sound like. I have used "slash" notation instead of actual notes so you can focus on the rhythm. To begin, use whatever voicings you are comfortable with to interpret the given chord symbols.

If you find it too difficult to play the comping pattern as written, then you can take any two- or four-bar section, learn the rhythms in that section, and repeat those rhythms over the entire form until you are comfortable with them. This will help you learn to play the entire sample comping pattern and will also cause you to become very proficient at playing in $\frac{3}{4}$ time. Eventually you will feel comfortable interacting with the soloist and creating comping patterns spontaneously in response to what the other musicians are doing.

This piece contains many Major 7th and Major 7#11 chords. It also utilizes other chords with which you should be familiar now, such as Dominant 7ths and Minor 7ths. After you learn the melody, try improvising over the solo form (section B). It may help you to write in the name of each scale you will be using. Here are some suggestions on how to break down your practicing to make it less overwhelming:

       solo with the right hand, with no left hand comping

       solo over one chord at a time until you are comfortable with that chord, both with left hand comping and without

       practice making the transition from one chord to the next by repeating a small section of two, three or four chords over and over

An audio file of this piece can be found on the Muse-Eek website under this book's title page. You can also find downloadable audio files and lead sheets of more of Roberta's compositions at www.robertajazz.com.

Just A Waltz

R. Piket

Further Exploration

The harmony used in this book is more advanced than that in some of the other books in this series. Below is a list of jazz music which goes beyond Be-bop harmony. Many of these recordings were made in the 1960's, in the post-modern era that followed the Be-bop era. In the discographies in the other volumes of this series, I focused on the great pianists. In this brief discography, the focus is on jazz compositon; specifically, the great jazz composers who helped revolutionize jazz harmony. (Note: There is some overlap with the piano discographies.)

You may wish to also utilize the discographies in Volumes 2 and 5 of this series. These focus more on piano performance than composition.

These discographies are also available on my website, www.robertajazz.com/discography.html, where they are frequently updated.

Post-Modern Jazz Harmony and Composition Sampler

Wayne Shorter
Etcetera (Blue Note)
The Soothsayer (Blue Note)
JuJu (EMI)

Miles Davis
Miles Smiles (Columbia)
Nefertiti (Columbia)
The Sorcerer (Columbia)
Filles De Kilimanjaro (Columbia)

George Russell
Ezz-Thetics (Original Jazz Classics)
The Stratus Seekers (Original Jazz Classics)

McCoy Tyner
The Real McCoy (Blue Note)

Chick Corea
Early Days (Delta, released in 1996)
The Song Of Singing (Capitol)

Herbie Hancock
The Prisoner (EMI)
Empyrean Isles (Blue Note)

Joe Henderson
In 'N Out (Blue Note)
Mode For Joe (Blue Note)
Inner Urge (Blue Note)

Bill Evans
Sunday At The Village Vanguard (Riverside)
The Paris Concert Edition 1 (Blue Note)
The Paris Concert Edition 2 (Blue Note)

What Next?

If you have mastered the material in this book you are on your way to becoming a versatile jazz pianist. You now have a grasp of some of the post-modern vocabulary of jazz. The exercises in this book are only a starting point which you can use in many different ways. You are now at the point in your learning where you should take greater responsibility for your musical growth by inventing your own variations on this material based on your needs.

This book is part of a series of books that focuses on learning and applying jazz scales in order to give you the vocabulary and confidence to become a fluid jazz improvisor. When you are ready, you may wish to build on the progress you've made by choosing another book in this series, such as *Volume 3, The Phrygian Mode*, which offers additional advanced harmonic material. (The volumes are ordered by their place relative to their parent scale, not by degree of difficulty. For example, the Phrygian mode starts on the third degree of the major scale and is therefore Volume 3, while the Lydian mode is the fourth mode of the major scale and is therefore Volume 4.)

If you have any questions or concerns about music that have not been addressed in this book, feel free to contact me through the FAQ page for this book at the Muse-Eek website, www.muse-eek.com. I wish you a rewarding musical journey.

Books Available From
Muse Eek Publishing Company

The Bruce Arnold series of instruction books for guitar are the result of 20 years of teaching. Mr. Arnold, who teaches at New York University and Princeton University has listened to the questions and problems of his students, and written fifty books addressing the needs of the beginning to advanced student. Written in a direct, friendly and practical manner, each book is structured in such a way as to enable a student to understand, retain and apply musical information. In short, these books teach.

1st Steps for a Beginning Guitarist
Spiral Bound ISBN 1890944-90-4   Perfect Bound ISBN 1890944-93-9

1st Steps for a Beginning Guitarist is a comprehensive method for guitar students who have no prior musical training. Whether you are playing acoustic, electric or twelve-string guitar, this book will give you the information you need, and trouble shoot the various pitfalls that can hinder the self-taught musician. Includes pictures, videos and audio in the form of midifiles and mp3's.

Chord Workbook for Guitar Volume 1 (2nd edition)
Spiral Bound ISBN 0-9648632-1-9   Perfect Bound ISBN 1890944-50-5

A consistent seller, this book addresses the needs of the beginning through intermediate student. The beginning student will learn chords on the guitar, and a section is also included to help learn the basics of music theory. Progressions are provided to help the student apply these chords to common sequences. The more advanced student will find the reharmonization section to be an invaluable resource of harmonic choices. Information is given through musical notation as well as tablature.

Chord Workbook for Guitar Volume 2 (2nd edition)
Spiral Bound ISBN 0-9648632-3-5   Perfect Bound ISBN 1890944-51-3

This book is the Rosetta Stone of pop/jazz chords, and is geared to the intermediate to advanced student. These are the chords that any serious student bent on a musical career must know. Unlike other books which simply give examples of isolated chords, this unique book provides a comprehensive series of progressions and chord combinations which are immediately applicable to both composition and performance.

Music Theory Workbook for Guitar Series

The worlds most popular instrument, the guitar, is not taught in our public schools. In addition, it is one of the hardest on which to learn the basics of music. As a result, it is frequently difficult for the serious guitarist to get a firm foundation in theory.

Theory Workbook for Guitar Volume 1
Spiral Bound ISBN 0-9648632-4-3   Perfect Bound ISBN 1890944-52-1

This book provides real hands-on application of intervals and chords. A theory section written in concise and easy to understand language prepares the student for all exercises. Worksheets are given that quiz a student about intervals and chord construction using staff notation and guitar tablature. Answers are supplied in the back of the book enabling a student to work without a teacher.

Theory Workbook for Guitar Volume 2
Spiral Bound ISBN 0-9648632-5-1   Perfect Bound ISBN 1890944-53-X

This book provides real hands-on application for 22 different scale types. A theory section written in concise and easy to understand language prepares the student for all exercises. Worksheets are given that quiz a student about scale construction using staff notation and guitar tablature. Answers are supplied in the back of the book enabling a student to work without a teacher. Audio files are also available on the muse-eek.com website to facilitate practice and improvisation with all the scales presented.

Rhythm Book Series

These books are a breakthrough in music instruction, using the internet as a teaching tool! Audio files of all the exercises are easily downloaded from the internet.

Rhythm Primer
Spiral Bound ISBN 0-890944-03-3   Perfect Bound ISBN 1890944-59-9

This 61 page book concentrates on all basic rhythms using four rhythmic levels. All examples use one pitch, allowing the student to focus completely on time and rhythm. All exercises can be downloaded from the internet to facilitate learning. See http://www.muse-eek.com for details

Rhythms Volume 1
Spiral Bound ISBN 0-9648632-7-8   Perfect Bound ISBN 1890944-55-6

This 120 page book concentrates on eighth note rhythms and is a thesaurus of rhythmic patterns. All examples use one pitch, allowing the student to focus completely on time and rhythm. All exercises can be downloaded from the internet to facilitate learning. See http://www.muse-eek.com for details.

Rhythms Volume 2
Spiral Bound ISBN 0-9648632-8-6   Perfect Bound ISBN 1890944-56-4

This volume concentrates on sixteenth note rhythms, and is a 108 page thesaurus of rhythmic patterns. All examples use one pitch, allowing the student to focus completely on time and rhythm. All exercises can be downloaded from the internet to facilitate learning. See http://www.muse-eek.com for details.

Rhythms Volume 3
Spiral Bound ISBN 0-890944-04-1   Perfect Bound ISBN 1890944-57-2

This volume concentrates on thirty second note rhythms, and is a 102 page thesaurus of rhythmic patterns. All examples use one pitch, allowing the student to focus completely on time and rhythm. All exercises can be downloaded from the internet to facilitate learning. See http://www.muse-eek.com for details.

Odd Meters Volume 1
Spiral Bound ISBN 0-9648632-9-4   Perfect Bound ISBN 1890944-58-0

This book applies both eighth and sixteenth note rhythms to odd meter combinations. All examples use one pitch, allowing the student to focus completely on time and rhythm. Exercises can be downloaded from the internet to facilitate learning. This 100 page book is an essential sight reading tool.
See http://www.muse-eek.com for details.

Contemporary Rhythms Volume 1
Spiral Bound ISBN 1-890944-27-0   Perfect Bound ISBN 1890944-84-X

This volume concentrates on eight note rhythms and is a thesaurus of rhythmic patterns. Each exercise uses one pitch which allows the student to focus completely on time and rhythm. Exercises use modern innovations common to twentieth century notation, thereby familiarizing the student with the most sophisticated systems likely to be encountered in the course of a musical career. All exercises can be downloaded from the internet to facilitate learning. See http://www.muse-eek.com for details.

Contemporary Rhythms Volume 2
Spiral Bound ISBN 1-890944-28-9   Perfect Bound ISBN 1890944-85-8

This volume concentrates on sixteenth note rhythms and is a thesaurus of rhythmic patterns. Each exercise uses one pitch which allows the student to focus completely on time and rhythm. Exercise use modern innovations common to twentieth century notation, thereby familiarizing the student with the most sophisticated systems likely to be encountered in the course of a musical career. All exercises can be downloaded from the internet to facilitate learning. See http://www.muse-eek.com for details.

Independence Volume 1
Spiral Bound ISBN 1-890944-00-9   Perfect Bound ISBN 1890944-83-1

This 51 page book is designed for pianists, stick and touchstyle guitarists, percussionists and anyone who wishes to develop the rhythmic independence of their hands. This volume concentrates on quarter, eighth and sixteenth note rhythms and is a thesaurus of rhythmic patterns. The exercises in this book gradually incorporate more and more complex rhythmic patterns making it an excellent tool for both the beginning and the advanced student.

Other Guitar Study Aids

Right Hand Technique for Guitar Volume 1
Spiral Bound ISBN 0-9648632-6-X   Perfect Bound ISBN 1890944-54-8

Heres a breakthrough in music instruction, using the internet as a teaching tool! This book gives a concise method for developing right hand technique on the guitar, one of the most overlooked and under-addressed aspects of learning the instrument. The simplest, most basic movements are used to build fatigue-free technique. Exercises can be downloaded from the internet to facilitate learning. See http://www.muse-eek.com for details.

Single String Studies Volume One
Spiral Bound ISBN 1-890944-01-7   Perfect Bound ISBN 1890944-62-9

This book is an excellent learning tool for both the beginner who has no experience reading music on the guitar, and the advanced student looking to improve their ledger line reading and general knowledge of each string of the guitar. Each exercise concentrates the students attention on one string at a time. This allows a familiarity to form between the written pitch and where it can be found on the guitar along with improving ones feel for jumping linearly across the fretboard. Exercises can be downloaded from the internet to facilitate learning. See http://www.muse-eek.com for details.

Single String Studies Volume Two
Spiral Bound ISBN 1-890944-05-X   Perfect Bound ISBN 1890944-64-5

This book is a continuation of Volume One, but using non-diatonic notes. Volume Two helps the intermediate and advanced student improve their ledger line reading and general knowledge of each string of the guitar. Each exercise concentrates the students attention on one string at a time. This allows a familiarity to form between the written pitch and where it can be found on the guitar along with improving ones feel for jumping linearly across the fretboard. Exercises can be downloaded from the internet to facilitate learning. See http://www.muse-eek.com for details.

Single String Studies Volume One (Bass Clef)
Spiral Bound ISBN 1-890944-02-5   Perfect Bound ISBN 1890944-63-7

This book is an excellent learning tool for both the beginner who has no experience reading music on the bass guitar, and the advanced student looking to improve their ledger line reading and general knowledge of each string of the bass. Each exercise concentrates a students attention of one string at a time. This allows a familiarity to form between the written pitch and where it can be found on the bass along with improving ones feel for jumping linearly across the fretboard. Exercises can be downloaded from the internet to facilitate learning. See http://www.muse-eek.com for details.

Single String Studies Volume Two (Bass Clef)
Spiral Bound ISBN 1-890944-06-8   Perfect Bound ISBN 1890944-65-3

This book is a continuation of Volume One, but using non-diatonic notes. Volume Two helps the intermediate and advanced student improve their ledger line reading and general knowledge of each string of the bass. Each exercise concentrates the students attention on one string at a time. This allows a familiarity to form between the written pitch and where it can be found on the bass along with improving ones feel for jumping linearly across the fretboard. Exercises can be downloaded from the internet to facilitate learning. See http://www.muse-eek.com for details.

Guitar Clinic
Spiral Bound ISBN 1-890944-45-9   Perfect Bound ISBN 1890944-86-6

Guitar Clinic contains techniques and exercises Mr. Arnold uses in the clinics and workshops he teaches around the U.S.. Much of the material in this book is culled from Mr. ArnoldÕs educational series, over thirty books in all. The student wishing to expand on his or her studies will find suggestions within the text as to which of Mr. Arnold's books will best serve their specific needs. Topics covered include: how to read music, sight reading, reading rhythms, music theory, chord and scale construction, modal sequencing, approach notes, reharmonization, bass and chord comping, and hexatonic scales.

The Essentials: Chord Charts, Scales, and Lead Patterns for the Guitar
Saddle Stitched (Stapled) ISBN 1-890944-94-7

This book is truly essential to the aspiring guitarist. It includes the most commonly played chords on the guitar in all keys, plus a bonus of the most commonly used scales and lead patterns. You can quickly learn all the chords, scales and lead patterns you need to know to play your favorite songs-and solo over them, too! The Essentials doesn't stop there, though. It also includes chord progressions to help you learn how to chord songs in folk, country, rock, blues and other popular styles. The books contain loads of easy to understand diagrams of chords, scales and lead patterns so you will be up and running in no time!

Sight Singing and Ear Training Series

The world is full of ear training and sight reading books, so why do we need more? This sight singing and ear training series uses a different method of teaching relative pitch sight singing and ear training. The success of this method has been remarkable. Along with a new method of ear training these books also use CDs and the internet as a teaching tool! Audio files of all the exercises are easily downloaded from the internet at www.muse-eek.com By combining interactive audio files with a new approach to ear training a studentÕs progress is limited only by their willingness to practice!

A Fanatic's Guide to Ear Training and Sight Singing
Spiral Bound ISBN 1-890944-19-X   Perfect Bound ISBN 1890944-75-0

This book and CD present a method for developing good pitch recognition through sight singing. This method differs from the myriad of other sight singing books in that it develops the ability to identify and name all twelve pitches within a key center. Through this method a student gains the ability to identify sound based on itÕs relationship to a key and not the relationship of one note to another (i.e. interval training as commonly taught in many texts). All note groupings from one to six notes are presented giving the student a thesaurus of basic note combinations which develops sight singing and note recognition to a level unattainable before this GuideÕs existence.

Key Note Recognition
Spiral Bound ISBN 1-890944-30-3   Perfect Bound ISBN 1890944-77-7

This book and CD present a method for developing the ability to recognize the function of any note against a key. This method is a must for anyone who wishes to sound one note on an instrument or voice and instantly know what key a song is in. Through this method a student gains the ability to identify a sound based on its relationship to a key and not the relationship of one note to another (i.e. interval training as commonly taught in many texts). Key Center Recognition is a definite requirement before proceeding to two note ear training.

LINES Volume One: Sight Reading and Sight Singing Exercises
Spiral Bound ISBN 1-890944-09-2   Perfect Bound ISBN 1890944-76-9

This book can be used for many applications. It is an excellent source for easy half note melodies that a beginner can use to learn how to read music or for sight singing slightly chromatic lines. An intermediate or advanced student will find exercises for multi-voice reading. These exercises can also be used for multi-voice ear training. The book has the added benefit in that all exercises can be heard by downloading the audio files for each example. See http://www.muse-eek.com for details.

LINES Volume Two: Sight Reading and Sight Singing Exercises
Spiral Bound ISBN 1-594899-88-6   Perfect Bound ISBN 1594899-99-1

Recommended for those who have completed volume one, volume two introduces more complex harmonic material. This book can be used for many applications. It is an excellent source for easy quarter note melodies that a beginner can use to learn how to read music or for sight singing slightly chromatic lines. An intermediate or advanced student will find exercises for multi-voice reading. These exercises can also be used for multi-voice ear training. The book has the added benefit in that all exercises can be heard by downloading the audio files for each example. See http://www.muse-eek.com for details.

Ear Training ONE NOTE: Beginning Level
Spiral Bound ISBN 1-890944-12-2   Perfect Bound ISBN 1890944-66-1

This Book and Audio CD presents a new and exciting method for developing relative pitch ear training. It has been used with great success and is now finally available on CD. There are three levels available depending on the student's ability. This beginning level is recommended for students who have little or no music training.

Ear Training ONE NOTE: Intermediate Level
Spiral Bound ISBN 1-890944-13-0   Perfect Bound ISBN 1890944-67-X

This Audio CD and booklet presents a new and exciting method of developing relative pitch ear training. It has been used with great success and is now finally available on CD. This intermediate level is recommended for students who have had some music training but still find their skills need more development.

Ear Training ONE NOTE: Advanced Level
Spiral Bound ISBN 1-890944-14-9   Perfect Bound ISBN 1890944-68-8

This Audio CD and booklet presents a new and exciting method of developing relative pitch ear training. It has been used with great success and is now finally available on CD. There are three levels available depending on the student's ability. This advanced level is recommended for students who have worked with the intermediate level and now wish to perfect their skills.

Ear Training TWO NOTE: Beginning Level Volume One
Spiral Bound ISBN 1-890944-31-9   Perfect Bound ISBN 1890944-69-6

This Book and Audio CD continues the method of developing relative pitch ear training as set forth in the "Ear Training, One Note" series. There are six volumes in the beginning level series. Through practice, the student eventually gains the ability to recognize the key and the names of any two notes played simultaneously. Volume One concentrates on 5ths. Prerequisite: a strong grasp of the One Note method.

Ear Training TWO NOTE: Beginning Level Volume Two
Spiral Bound ISBN 1-890944-32-7   Perfect Bound ISBN 1890944-70-X

This Book and Audio CD continues the method of developing relative pitch ear training as set forth in the "Ear Training, One Note" series. There are six volumes in the beginning level series. Through practice, the student eventually gains the ability to recognize the key and the names of any two notes played simultaneously. Volume Two concentrates on 3rds. Prerequisite: a strong grasp of the One Note method.

Ear Training TWO NOTE: Beginning Level Volume Three
Spiral Bound ISBN 1-890944-33-5   Perfect Bound ISBN 1890944-71-8

This Book and Audio CD continues the method of developing relative pitch ear training as set forth in the "Ear Training, One Note" series. There are six volumes in the beginning level series. Through practice, the student eventually gains the ability to recognize the key and the names of any two notes played simultaneously. Volume Three concentrates on 6ths. Prerequisite: a strong grasp of the One Note method.

Ear Training TWO NOTE: Beginning Level Volume Four
Spiral Bound ISBN 1-890944-34-3   Perfect Bound ISBN 1890944-72-6

This Book and Audio CD continues the method of developing relative pitch ear training as set forth in the "Ear Training, One Note" series. There are six volumes in the beginning level series. Through practice, the student eventually gains the ability to recognize the key and the names of any two notes played simultaneously. Volume Four concentrates on 4ths. Prerequisite: a strong grasp of the One Note method.

Ear Training TWO NOTE: Beginning Level Volume Five
Spiral Bound ISBN 1-890944-35-1   Perfect Bound ISBN 1890944-73-4

This Book and Audio CD continues the method of developing relative pitch ear training as set forth in the "Ear Training, One Note" series. There are six volumes in the beginning level series. Through practice, the student eventually gains the ability to recognize the key and the names of any two notes played simultaneously. Volume Five concentrates on 2nds. Prerequisite: a strong grasp of the One Note method.

Ear Training TWO NOTE: Beginning Level Volume Six
Spiral Bound ISBN 1-890944-36-X   Perfect Bound ISBN 1890944-74-2

This Book and Audio CD continues the method of developing relative pitch ear training as set forth in the "Ear Training, One Note" series. There are six volumes in the beginning level series. Through practice, the student eventually gains the ability to recognize the key and the names of any two notes played simultaneously. Volume Six concentrates on 7ths. Prerequisite: a strong grasp of the One Note method.

Comping Styles Series

This series is built on the progressions found in Chord Workbook Volume One. Each book covers a specific style of music and presents exercises to help a guitarist, bassist or drummer master that style. Audio CDs are also available so a student can play along with each example and really get "into the groove."

Comping Styles for the Guitar Volume Two FUNK
Spiral Bound ISBN 1-890944-07-6   Perfect Bound ISBN 1890944-60-2

This volume teaches a student how to play guitar or piano in a funk style. 36 Progressions are presented: 12 keys of a Major and Minor Blues plus 12 keys of Rhythm Changes A different groove is presented for each exercise giving the student a wide range of funk rhythms to master. An Audio CD is also included so a student can play along with each example and really get "into the groove." The audio CD contains "trio" versions of each exercise with Guitar, Bass and Drums.

Comping Styles for the Bass Volume Two FUNK
Spiral Bound ISBN 1-890944-08-4   Perfect Bound ISBN 1890944-61-0

This volume teaches a student how to play bass in a funk style. 36 Progressions are presented: 12 keys of a Major and Minor Blues plus 12 keys of Rhythm Changes A different groove is presented for each exercise giving the student a wide range of funk rhythms to master. An Audio CD is also included so a student can play along with each example and really get "into the groove." The audio CD contains "trio" versions of each exercise with Guitar, Bass and Drums.

Jazz and Blues Bass Line
Spiral Bound ISBN 1-890944-15-7   Perfect Bound ISBN 1890944-16-5

This book covers the basics of bass line construction. A theoretical guide to building bass lines is presented along with 36 chord progressions utilizing the twelve keys of a Major and Minor Blues, plus twelve keys of Rhythm Changes. A reharmonization section is also provided which demonstrates how to reharmonize a chord progression on the spot.

Time Series

The Doing Time series presents a method for contacting, developing and relying on your internal time sense: This series is an excellent resource for any musician who is serious about developing strong internal sense of time. This is particularly useful in any kind of music where the rhythms and time signatures may be very complex or free, and there is no conductor.

THE BIG METRONOME
Spiral Bound ISBN 1-890944-37-8   Perfect Bound ISBN 1890944-82-3

The Big Metronome is designed to help you develop a better internal sense of time. This is accomplished by requiring you to "feel time" rather than having you rely on the steady click of a metronome. The idea is to slowly wean yourself away from an external device and rely on your internal/natural sense of time. The exercises presented work in conjunction with the three CDs that accompany this book. CD 1 presents the first 13 settings from a traditional metronome 40-66; the second CD contains metronome markings 69-116, and the third CD contains metronome markings 120-208. The first CD gives you a 2 bar count off and a click every measure, the second CD gives you a 2 bar count off and a click every 2 measures, the 3rd CD gives you a 2 bar count off and a click every 4 measures. By presenting all common metronome markings a student can use these 3 CDs as a replacement for a traditional metronome.

Doing Time with the Blues Volume One:
Spiral Bound ISBN 1-890944-17-3   Perfect Bound ISBN 1890944-78-5

The book and CD presents a method for gaining an internal sense of time thereby eliminating dependence on a metronome. The book presents the basic concept for developing good time and also includes exercises that can be practiced with the CD. The CD provides eight 8 minute tracks at different tempos in which the time is delineated every 2 bars, and with an extra hit every 12 bars to outline the blues form. The student may then use the exercises presented in the book to gain control of their execution or improvise to gain control of their ideas using this bare minimum of time delineation.

Doing Time with the Blues Volume Two:
Spiral Bound ISBN 1-890944-18-1   Perfect Bound ISBN 1890944-79-3

This is the 2nd volume of a four volume series which presents a method for developing a musicians internal sense of time, thereby eliminating dependence on a metronome. This 2nd volume presents different exercises which further the development of this time sense. This 2nd volume begins to test even a professional level players ability. The CD provides eight 8 minute tracks at different tempos in which the time is delineated every 4 bars with an extra hit every 12 bars to outline the blues form. New exercises are also included that can be practiced with the CD. This series is an excellent resource for any musician who is serious about developing an internal sense of time.

Doing Time with 32 bars Volume One:
Spiral Bound ISBN 1-890944-22-X   Perfect Bound ISBN Spiral Bound ISBN 1890944-80-7

The book and CD presents a method for gaining an internal sense of time thereby eliminating dependence on a metronome. The book presents the basic concept for developing good time and also includes exercises that can be practiced with the CD. The CD provides eight 8 minute tracks at different tempos in which the time is delineated every 2 bars, with an extra hit every 32 to outline the 32 bar form. The student may then use the exercises presented in the book to gain control of their execution or improvise to gain control of their ideas using this bare minimum of time delineation.

Doing Time with 32 bars Volume Two:
Spiral Bound ISBN 1-890944-23-8   Perfect Bound ISBN Spiral Bound ISBN 1890944-81-5

This is the 2nd volume of a four volume series which presents a method for developing a musicians internal sense of time, thereby eliminating dependence on a metronome.. This 2nd volume presents different exercises which further the development of this time sense. This 2nd volume begins to test even a professional level players ability. The CD provides eight 8 minute tracks at different tempos in which the time is delineated every 4 bars with an extra hit every 32 bars to outline the 32 bar form. New exercises are also included that can be practiced with the CD. This series is an excellent resource for any musician who is serious about developing an internal sense of time.

Other Workbooks

Music Theory Workbook for All Instruments, Volume 1: Interval and Chord Construction
Spiral Bound ISBN 1594899-51-7   Perfect Bound ISBN 1890944-46-7

This book provides real hands-on application of intervals and chords. A theory section written in concise and easy to understand language prepares the student for all exercises. Worksheets are given that quiz a student about intervals and chord construction using staff notation. Answers are supplied in the back of the book enabling a student to work without a teacher.

Jazz Piano Vocabulary by Roberta Piket, Volume 1: The Major Scale
Spiral Bound ISBN 1594899-51-7   Perfect Bound ISBN 1594899-51-7

This is the 1st volume in a series designed to help the student of jazz piano learn and apply jazz scales by mastering each scale and its uses in improvisation. Each book focuses on a different scale, illustrating the scale in all twelve keys with complete fingerings. Also provided are chords and left hand voicings to match, exercises and études to apply the material to improvising, ideas for further study and listening, and detailed suggestions on how to prace the material. Volume 1 also includes a detailed primer in note reading, basic theory, and rhythmic notation.

Jazz Piano Vocabulary by Roberta Piket, Volume 2: The Dorian Mode
Spiral Bound ISBN 1890944-96-3   Perfect Bound ISBN 1890944-98-X

The 2nd volume in the series, this book focuses on the Dorian scale and applies it to improvising on minor seventh chords. The Dorian scale is presented in all twelve keys with complete fingerings. The book also contains left hand voicings, exercises, many examples, an étude to help apply the material, ideas for further study, an extended discography, and detailed instruction and practice tips.

Jazz Piano Vocabulary by Roberta Piket, Volume 3: The Phrygian Mode
Spiral Bound ISBN 1594899-53-3   Perfect Bound ISBN 1594899-54-1

For students who have covered the basics in Volume 1,2 and 5, this book focuses in the Phrygian and Spanish Phrygian scales. It discusses "modern" jazz chords such as the "Phrygian" chord (susb9). The scale is presented in all 12 keys with fingerings. It also provides a detailed treatise on a modal approach to chord voicings, practice tips and a Phrygian étude.

Jazz Piano Vocabulary by Roberta Piket, Volume 4: The Lydian Mode
Spiral Bound ISBN 1594899-55-X   Perfect Bound ISBN 1594899-56-8

Volume 4 focuses on the Lydian mode in all twelve keys with fingerings. Chords are presented with left-hand voicings that work with the mode. Also included are exercises to help the intermediate improvisor with common phrasing and rhythmic problems, a jazz waltz etude with suggested $\frac{3}{4}$ comping patterns, comping exercises and examples from the masters, a study of major7th#11 and ♭5 chords, and a brief treatise on building fourths-based voicings. Because the Lydian mode is used in a more advanced harmonic context than some of the other modes, Vol. 4 is recommended after Volumes 1, 2, and 5 has been mastered. Added feature: the author can be contacted online.

Jazz Piano Vocabulary by Roberta Piket, Volume 5: The Mixolydian Mode
Spiral Bound ISBN 1594899-57-6   Perfect Bound ISBN 1594899-58-4

This book focuses on the Mixolydian scale and applies it to improvising on dominant seventh and dominant seventh sus chords. The scale is presented in all twelve keys with fingerings. The book also contains an introduction to approach notes, an explanation and etude on twelve bar blues form, left hand voicings, exercises, melodic examples, instruction and practice tips.

The New York Guitar Method Book 1
Spiral Bound ISBN 159489-987-8   Perfect Bound ISBN 159489-900-2

  This series of books distills several of our previous publications into a method currently in use at New York University for the Summer Guitar Intensive Program. Content is geared towards both the straight ahead player seeking to understand previous styles of playing, or the avant-garde enthusiast looking to expand into uncharted territory. Material concentrates on essential information the student must master in order to become a professional guitarist in the heavily competitive New York City music scene. While the book is set up as a 3 week intensive course of study for NYU, it can also be used as the basis for a regular 15 week semester program, should others wish to use it in that manner. Additional features facilitate its use by teachers as well as students studying on their own. This resource consists of a DVD, two Ear Training CDs, and a Chord Vamps CD, all included in each book.

The New York Guitar Method Book 2
Spiral Bound ISBN 159489-901-0   Perfect Bound ISBN 159489-902-9

   This is the second book in our series currently in use at New York University for the Summer Guitar Intensive Program. A continuation of Volume 1, Volume 2 focuses on approach notes and discusses how to apply approaches to jazz lines in order to create the signature sounding lines of bebop through the contemporary sounding lines of the modern masters.

The New York Guitar Method Book 3
Spiral Bound ISBN 159489-903-7   Perfect Bound ISBN 159489-904-5

  This is the third book in our series currently in use at New York University for the Summer Guitar Intensive Program. A continuation of Volume 2, Volume 3 focuses on 2 and 3 note structures and how to apply them in improvisation and composition.

The New York Guitar Method Ensemble Book 1
Spiral Bound ISBN 159489-905-3   Perfect Bound ISBN 159489-906-1

   This series of books combines many of our previous publications into a method currently in use at New York University for their Summer Guitar Intensive Program. Our Ensemble Method presents a breakthrough approach for teaching guitarists how to sightread. Each chapter has eighth note, sixteenth note, single string, lines, and chord exercises. The book also includes jazz and classical reading études and is an excellent resource for lab/ensemble studies as it contains 3 and 4-part reading examples.

The New York Guitar Method Ensemble Book 2
Spiral Bound ISBN 159489-907-X   Perfect Bound ISBN 159489-908-8

   A contuation of Volume One, Volume Two focuses on reading jazz solos that demonstrate the many uses of approach notes as discussed in the accompanying New York Guitar Method Volume 2. The book also includes jazz and classical reading études and is an excellent resource for lab/ensemble studies as it contains 3 and 4-part reading examples.

The New York Guitar Method Ensemble Book 3
Spiral Bound ISBN 159489-909-6   Perfect Bound ISBN 159489-910-X

   A contuation of Volume Two, Volume Three focuses on reading jazz solos that highlight the many uses of two and three note pitch class sets as discussed in the accompanying New York Guitar Method Volume 3. The book also includes jazz and classical reading études and is an excellent resource for lab/ensemble studies as it contains 3 and 4-part reading examples.

The New York Guitar Method Primer Book 1
Spiral Bound ISBN 159489-911-8   Perfect Bound ISBN 159489-912-6

   This book provides students with an excellent foundation in theory, ear training, chord and scale comprehension on the guitar. It is a prerequisite for entering New York University's Summer Guitar Intensive Program and provides students studying independently with the tools they will need to successfully move on to Primer Book 2.

The New York Guitar Method Primer Book 2
Spiral Bound ISBN 159489-91-0   Perfect Bound ISBN 159489-916-9

   This book provides students with an excellent foundation in theory, ear training, chord and scale comprehension on the guitar. It is a prerequisite for entering New York University's Summer Guitar Intensive Program and provides students studying independently with the tools they will need to successfully move on to New York Guitar Method Book 1.

The New York Guitar Method Primer Ensemble Book 2
Spiral Bound ISBN 159489-913-4   Perfect Bound ISBN 159489-914-2

   This book is a prerequisite for entering New York University's Summer Guitar Intensive Program and provides students studying independently with the tools they will need to successfully move on to Volume 1. Our Ensemble Method presents a breakthrough approach for teaching guitarist how to sightread. Each chapter has eighth note, sixteenth note, single string, lines, and chord exercises. The book also includes modal jazz vamps and solos and is an excellent resource for lab/ensemble studies as it contains 3 and 4-part reading examples.

E-Books

The Bruce Arnold series of instructional E-books is for the student who wishes to target specific areas of study that are of particular interest. Many of these books are excerpted from other larger texts. The excerpted source is listed for each book. These books are available on-line at www.muse-eek.com as well as at many e-tailers throughout the internet. These books can also be purchased in the traditional book binding format. (See the ISBN number for proper format)

Chord Velocity: Volume One, Learning to switch between chords quickly
E-book ISBN 1-890944-88-2   Traditional Book Binding ISBN 1-890944-97-1

The first hurdle a beginning guitarist encounters is difficulty in switching between chords quickly enough to make a chord progression sound like music. This book provides exercises that help a student gradually increase the speed with which they change chords. Special free audio files are also available on the muse-eek.com website to make practice more productive and fun. Within a few weeks, remarkable improvement can be achieved using this method. This book is excerpted from "1st Steps for a Beginning Guitarist Volume One."

Guitar Technique: Volume One, Learning the basics to fast, clean, accurate and fluid performance skills.
E-book ISBN 1-890944-91-2   Traditional Book Binding ISBN 1-890944-99-8

This book is for both the beginning guitarist or the more experienced guitarist who wishes to improve their technique. All aspects of the physical act of playing the guitar are covered, from how to hold a guitar to the specific way each hand is involved in the playing process. Pictures and videos are provided to help clarify each technique. These pictures and videos are either contained in the book or can be downloaded at www.muse-eek.com This book is excerpted from "1st Steps for a Beginning Guitarist Volume One."

Accompaniment: Volume One, Learning to Play Bass and Chords Simultaneously
E-book ISBN 1-890944-87-4   Traditional Book Binding ISBN 1-890944-96-3

The techniques found within this book are an excellent resource for creating and understanding how to play bass and chords simultaneously in a jazz or blues style. Special attention is paid to understanding how this technique is created, thereby enabling the student to recreate this style with other pieces of music. This book is excerpted from the book "Guitar Clinic."

Beginning Rhythm Studies: Volume One, Learning the basics of reading rhythm and playing in time.
E-book ISBN 1-890944-89-0   Traditional Book Binding 1-890944-98-X

This book covers the basics for anyone wishing to understand or improve their rhythmic abilities. Simple language is used to show the student how to read and play rhythm. Exercises are presented which can accelerate the learning process. Audio examples in the form of midifiles are available on the muse-eek.com website to facilitate learning the correct rhythm in time. This book is excerpted from the book "Rhythm Primer."

www.ingramcontent.com/pod-product-compliance
Lightning Source LLC
LaVergne TN
LVHW061318060426
835507LV00019B/2208